MAR 2013

Latinos Today

Hispanic Americans: Major Minority

Latinos Today

Thomas Arkham

Mason Crest

Mason Crest
370 Reed Road
Broomall, Pennsylvania 19008
www.masoncrest.com

Printed and bound in the United States of America.

First printing
9 8 7 6 5 4 3 2 1

Library of Congress Cataloging-in-Publication Data

Arkham, Thomas.
 Latinos today / by Thomas Arkham.
    p. cm.
 ISBN 978-1-4222-2327-7 (hardcover) — ISBN 978-1-4222-2315-4 (hardcover series) — ISBN 978-1-4222-9331-7 (ebook)
 1. Hispanic Americans—Juvenile literature. I. Title.
 E184.S75A87 2013
 973'.0468—dc23
                          2012010664

Produced by Harding House Publishing Services, Inc.
www.hardinghousepages.com
Interior design by Micaela Sanna.
Cover design by Torque Advertising + Design.
Printed in USA.

Contents

Introduction

by José E. Limón, Ph.D.

Even before there was a United States, Hispanics were present in what would become this country. Beginning in the sixteenth century, Spanish explorers traversed North America, and their explorations encouraged settlement as early as the sixteenth century in what is now northern New Mexico and Florida, and as late as the mid-eighteenth century in what is now southern Texas and California.

Later, in the nineteenth century, following Spain's gradual withdrawal from the New World, Mexico in particular established its own distinctive presence in what is now the southwestern part of the United States, a presence reinforced in the first half of the twentieth century by substantial immigration from that country. At the close of the nineteenth century, the U.S. war with Spain brought Cuba and Puerto Rico into an interactive relationship with the United States, the latter in a special political and economic affiliation with the United States even as American power influenced the course of almost every other Latin American country.

The books in this series remind us of these historical origins, even as each explores the present reality of different Hispanic groups. Some of these books explore the contemporary social origins—what social scientists call the "push" factors—behind the accelerating Hispanic immigration to America: political instability, economic underdevelopment and crisis, environmental degradation, impoverished or wholly absent educational systems, and other circumstances contribute to many Latin Americans deciding they will be better off in the United States.

And, for the most part, they will be. The vast majority come to work and work very hard, in order to earn better wages than they would back home. They fill significant labor needs in the U.S. economy and contribute to the economy through lower consumer prices and sales taxes.

When they leave their home countries, many immigrants may initially fear that they are leaving behind vital and important aspects of their home cultures: the Spanish language, kinship ties, food, music, folklore, and the arts. But as these books also make clear, culture is a fluid thing, and these native cultures are not only brought to America, they are also replenished in the United States in fascinating and novel ways. These books further suggest to us that Hispanic groups enhance American culture as a whole.

Our country—especially the young, future leaders who will read these books—can only benefit by the fair and full knowledge these authors provide about the socio-historical origins and contemporary cultural manifestations of America's Hispanic heritage.

chapter 1
LATINOS IN THE UNITED STATES

The United States is made up of a lot of different people. Over the past 500 years, people from all over the world came to America. People from just about every corner of the globe are here now.

One of the biggest groups of people that call the United States home are Latinos. Latinos are people that come from Latin America. In the United States, we call people from Latin American countries Latinos. Lots of people from Latin America have come to the United States. Some came a long time ago. Many more have come in the last few years. Each year, more and more Latinos arrive in the United States.

A Lot of Variety

The word Latino refers to a lot of different people. A Latino could be from any country in Latin America. There are a lot of countries there. They are all different. They have different histories. Some are thousands of miles apart. That means Latinos can be very different from each other.

Sometimes people like to be identified by the country from which they came. So, instead of "Latino," we could say "Guatemalan" or "Peruvian." Each country is different from the next. People don't always like to be all lumped into the term "Latino."

Everyone from Latin America is different. For example, most Latinos speak Spanish. But not all. In the United States, some Latinos only know English. Their families have been here a long time. They don't use Spanish anymore. Other people from Latin American don't speak Spanish at all. People from Brazil speak Portuguese. People whose families are native speak **native** languages like Quechua.

Latinos all look different. Some have dark skin and black hair. Others are blond and blue-eyed. There are Latinos of every kind in between.

Not all Latinos eat the same food or listen to the same music. They don't all practice the same religion.

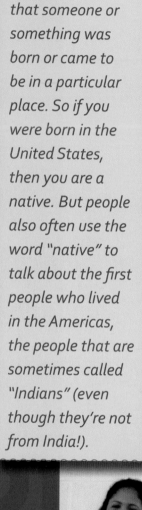

Native *means that someone or something was born or came to be in a particular place. So if you were born in the United States, then you are a native. But people also often use the word "native" to talk about the first people who lived in the Americas, the people that are sometimes called "Indians" (even though they're not from India!).*

Some Basic Geography

The American continents are big. They include North and South America. Central America is the skinny piece of land that connects North and South America.

North America is where the United States is. To the north of the United States is Canada. To the south is Mexico. Mexico is part of Latin America, even though it's in North America.

Directly south of North America is a piece of land called Central America. There are a few small countries here. They are also part of Latin America. Directly south of Central

WHAT IS LATIN AMERICA?

The Spanish-speaking countries in North and South America are called Latin America. Brazil is also considered part of Latin America, although the people there speak Portuguese.

Mexico

Guatemala

El Salvador

Honduras

Nicaragua

Costa Rica

Panama

Cuba

Dominican Republic

Venezuela

Colombia

Ecuador

Peru

Bolivia

Paraguay

Uruguay

Argentina

Chile

Puerto Rico (part of the United States)

Brazil

America is South America. Many more Latin American countries are here.

There is one more part of Latin America. Many small islands lie to the south of the United States. They are in the Caribbean Sea. Many of those islands are considered part of Latin America.

chapter 2
A HISTORY LESSON

Latino history has a lot of chapters. Some of those chapters are violent. Some are heroic. Some are peaceful. Latin American has had a lot going on!

A Long History

The only people who lived in North and South America used to be the people who were here before the Europeans arrived—the Natives. There were all kinds of Native people. There were hundreds of different groups.

The Americas is a big place. People made their homes in the Andes mountains in South America. They lived in the grass plains of North America. They lived on islands in the Caribbean.

All these people built different sorts of **cultures**. They had different languages. Some farmed, and some hunted animals and gathered wild foods. They had different religions. They made different music.

For a while, people in the Americas stayed there. People in Europe stayed in Europe. Then all that changed.

> **Cultures** *are the ways that different groups think about the world. Culture included language, food, art, customs, and religion.*

13

In 1492, Europeans came to the Americas. They sailed all the way across the ocean. Christopher Columbus and his crew landed first on the island of Hispañola in the Caribbean. (Today the countries of Haiti and the Dominican Republic are on that island.)

The Europeans didn't just come to look around. They came to take over. They wanted gold. They wanted slaves too.

Soon explorers and *conquistadors* (conquerors) were coming to the Americas. They traveled all over. Some went to South America, others to North America, and others to Central America.

> **Descendants** *are a person's children, grandchildren, great-grandchildren, and so on.*

The Europeans had better weapons than the Native people. The Europeans brought disease with them. Both of those things killed the people who already lived in the Americans. The Europeans destroyed a lot of Native groups.

But not all the Native people died. The Natives and the Europeans mixed. Babies were born with one parent from one culture and one parent from another.

Africans also came to the Americas. The Europeans brought them over as slaves. The Africans mixed with the Natives and the Europeans too.

This mix of people became the Latinos. Latinos today are the **descendants** of lots of different cultures and groups.

LATINOS TODAY

Mexican Americans

Mexican-Americans make up the biggest number of Latinos in the United States. Over half of all Latinos in the United States are Mexican.

How did they all get to the United States? Some have been here for many **generations**. Others have come recently.

A long time ago, in the 1800s, the United States fought the Mexican-American War. The United States wanted Mexican land. The United States won the war. Mexico signed the Guadalupe Hidalgo **Treaty.** The treaty took land away from Mexico. It gave it to the United States. The United States got Texas, Arizona, New Mexico, California, Utah, and Nevada.

All the people who lived in those lands used to be Mexican. Now they were Mexican American. Just like that!

Other people lived on the land too. They were the Native people who had lived there for centuries.

But now white Americans moved to the same land. They wanted the land for themselves. They didn't always like the Mexican Americans. The whites often treated the Mexican Americans and Natives badly.

Some of these Mexican Americans stayed in the area anyway. They worked on farms and ranches. Some moved to other parts of the United States, though. They went to work in big cities.

Then in the 1900s, more Mexicans crossed the border into the United States. They mostly came to find work on farms in the West. Some moved to the United States permanently. More came just to work. They still lived in Mexico, but they crossed the border to work.

Generations *are groups of people all born around the same time. Your grandparents belong to one generation. Your parents and aunts and uncles belong to another generation. And you, your brothers and sisters, and your cousins belong to another generation.*

*A **treaty** is a written agreement between two countries.*

During the **Great Depression**, fewer **immigrants** came. The United States even forced some Mexicans and Mexican-Americans to move back to Mexico.

But more immigrants came during World War II. People needed workers. And Mexicans needed work. Almost all of the Mexicans who crossed the border into America worked on big farms growing food.

Today there are millions of Mexican Americans. More continue to immigrate all the time. Many are illegal. That means they don't have permission from the U.S. government to live in the United States. But they cross the border anyway.

More than half of all Mexican Americans were born in the United States. Their families came here before they were born. They are U.S. **citizens.** Lots still live in the Southwest, especially in Texas.

Puerto Ricans

Puerto Rico is an island south of Florida. It is part of the United States (but it's not a state). People who come to the United States from Puerto Rico aren't immigrants. They don't need any special papers. They are part of this country. Puerto Ricans are American citizens.

The United States took control of Puerto Rico after the Spanish-American War. During the 1800s, Spain still ruled a lot of countries in Latin America. Cuba was one of them. But Cubans wanted to be free from Spain.

The United States sent a ship to Cuba, to keep an eye on things. Then the ship blew up. No one knew if it was an accident, or if Spain did it. The United States declared war on Spain.

After four months of war, Spain gave up. It gave its Caribbean islands to the United States. Now the islands had a new country that controlled them.

The United States took over the sugarcane farms in Puerto Rico. America made a lot of money off from sugarcane. English became Puerto Rico's second language. Puerto Ricans became United States citizens.

Lots of Puerto Ricans moved to the United States after World War II. Life could be hard in Puerto Rico. Jobs were hard to find. People wanted to find better lives in the United States. And it was easy to come here. They just had to get on a plane.

Life in the United States wasn't easy, though. Puerto Ricans sometimes had a hard time finding houses and jobs in the United States. The jobs most Puerto Rican could find didn't pay much. Other Americans didn't always like Puerto Ricans.

Some Puerto Ricans went back to their island. But many stayed. Today, New York City is home to a lot of Puerto Ricans. Puerto Ricans live in other places across the United States as well.

A HISTORY LESSON

Fidel Castro

Cubans

Cuba is another island south of Florida. In the 1950s, there was a **revolution** in Cuba. The government changed a lot.

A man named Fidel Castro took over. Not all Cubans liked that he was their leader. So these Cubans left.

At first, the people who left tended to be educated. They had some money. Most immigrants usually don't have much money or education. That's the reason they want to leave in the first place. But this group of people were leaving Cuba because they didn't like Castro.

Later, poorer Cubans came. They, too, wanted to get away from the government.

Cubans were welcomed to the United States. Americans didn't like Fidel Castro either. They were glad to help out people who also didn't like him. The United States gave them things. They gave them help finding homes. They trained them for jobs. Immigrants from other countries didn't get these things.

Most Cubans ended up in Miami, Florida. Lots of Cubans still live there. Whole neighborhoods are entirely Cuban. They own banks and factories. They work in construction. They own homes. They are doing very well.

> A **revolution** *is when the people get rid of their government and put their own government in its place.*

SPANISH NAMES

Did you know that a lot of place names in the United States come from Spanish? Five states are actually Spanish words: California (named by the conquistador Hernan Cortés after a place in a popular Spanish poem), Colorado (red colored), Florida (flowery), Montana (mountain), and Nevada (snow-covered).

Lots of cities and towns also have Spanish names. Los Angeles means "The Angels." San Francisco means "Saint Francis," a famous man in the Catholic religion. There are hundreds more examples.

Other Latinos

Mexicans, Puerto Ricans, and Cubans are the largest Latino groups in the United States. But millions more Latinos from other countries also live in the United States.

El Salvadoran immigrants are running away from hard times in their country. Lots of Dominican and Guatemalan immigrants also live in the United States. Smaller numbers of people from other countries have come too. All of these people are from Central America.

Other immigrants are from South America. They are mostly from Colombia and Ecuador. They are running away from problems with their government. They want to escape poverty and violence.

Once all these immigrants come to the United States, they can live anywhere. They spread out over the whole United States. However, immigrants often want to move to a city or town where people from their country already live. More South Americans live in California, Florida, and New York. They know people there. There are neighborhoods full of Latinos. So they move there.

Lots of Latinos

Latinos are the biggest **minority** group in the United States. They might soon be the biggest group in general. There are millions and millions of Latinos. Some are recent immigrants. They just got here. Some have families who have been here for a long time.

We can find the most Latinos in cities. Lots of Latinos live in New York City, Los Angeles, Houston, San Diego, Miami, and other cities. In some cities, Latinos make up more than half of all the people who live there.

Latinos also live in small cities. In Holland, Michigan, for example, most people are Latino. Holland used to be home to mostly Dutch people, but now that's changed. Puerto Ricans, Cubans, and Mexicans call Reading, Penn-

> A **minority** *is a smaller group within a larger group. The smaller group is different in some way from the rest of the larger group.*

A multi-generation Hispanic family

20

HISPANIC OR LATINO?

In the 1980s, the U.S. government came up with the name "Hispanic" for people who speak Spanish and live in the United States. Not everyone likes this name. Many people don't like the way the term lumps everyone together based only on language. The people in North and South America who speak Spanish have a very different culture from Spain's. Other people use the word "Latino" for this same group of people. They like this word better because it has more to do with Latin America than with Spain.

The fact that Hispanics—or Latinos—don't agree on which term to use for themselves shows how different they all are. They come from many different countries. They have different stories. But at the same time, Hispanic American cultures have many things in common. They share many of the same stories. They often worship God the same way. Many of the same things are important to them. They are proud of their art and music. They celebrate the same holidays.

sylvania, home. Nashville, Tennessee, is the center of country music—and now it has three Spanish-language radio stations.

Why are there so many Latinos? One reason is that they keep moving to the United States. More immigrants come every year.

Another reason is because Latinos often have big families. They have lots of kids. Each one of those kids grows up and has more kids. The United States government thinks there will be 80 million Latinos by 2050!

chapter 3
LATINO HEROES

Latinos have been heroes for thousands of people. Both Latinos and non-Latinos admire many of these heroes. Some have lived south of the border and some have lived in the United States. Latinos today still tell their stories. These heroes are a part of Latino culture. Their stories help shape Latinos today.

Robin Hoods

After the treaty that ended the Mexican American War, lots of Mexicans suddenly lived in the United States. Not everyone was happy about that. Whites who lived there wanted the land. They often treated the Mexican Americans badly.

Some Mexican Americans fought back. They robbed from rich, white people. Then they gave the money to poor Mexican folk—like England's Robin Hood.

White landowners hated the robbers. The poor in the area loved them though. They wrote songs and stories about them. They still sing them today.

Joaquin Muerrieta was one of the most famous robbers, or *banditos*. Most of his life is a mystery. So many stories have been told that no one knows what's true.

Murrieta worked in the mines in California. He was beaten up by whites. He was angry. He gathered up a group of men. Then they went out and fought the whites. He was eventually captured and killed.

Tiburcio Vásquez is another *bandito*. He didn't like how Mexican Americans were treated. He went around trying to protect them. He and his men robbed a bank in Arizona. They were trying to get money to raise an army. The townspeople came out and shot at Vásquez. He escaped, but now he was a wanted man. After running from the police for a long time, he was caught and hanged.

Pancho Villa

 ## Francisco "Pancho" Villa

Pancho Villa was a famous Mexican outlaw. He is a legend both in Mexico and in the United States. He was a cowboy who helped start a revolution.

Villa was born in Durango, Mexico, in 1877. His family worked on a ranch. When he was 16, he shot the ranch owner's son. Then he ran away so he wouldn't get in trouble.

He met up with some other men. Together, they robbed for a living. They eventually joined some Mexican rebels. After a while, Villa ended up creating an army of thousands of people. They fought the Mexican Revolution against Spain.

Villa was basically a king. He ruled land in Mexico. There, he made the rules. He stole cattle. He even made his own money.

Villa took money away from the rich and gave to the poor. He was yet another Mexican Robin Hood. But he was also cruel. He shot people for no reason. He did a lot of killing whenever people didn't agree with him.

Villa was also sort of a movie star. Americans were fascinated by him. They wanted to find out more. So filmmakers went to Mexico and filmed him. Villa staged battles just for them.

Then the United States got involved in the Mexican Revolution. They weren't on Villa's side. So he fought back. He raided American towns. He killed Americans. The army spent a long time chasing him. They couldn't catch him.

Mural of Pancho Villa

The government couldn't fight Villa. But they could pay him to stop fighting—so they did. He settled down on a ranch. In the end, though, he was killed by people who didn't like him.

José Martí

José Martí is a famous Cuban hero. He was born in Havana, the capital of Cuba, in 1853. At the time, Cuba was part of Spain.

Martí wanted his land to be free. He didn't want Spain to rule Cuba. When he was just 16, he was arrested for his ideas. He had to leave Cuba.

While he was gone, Martí traveled around the world. He went to Spain and the United States. He went to other Latin American countries. Everywhere he went, he talked to people about Cuban **independence**. He ended up living in New York City.

Martí was also a poet. He wrote many famous poems. Some talked about Cuban independence.

Eventually, he went back to Cuba. He wanted to be part of the actual fight against Spain. So he gathered together a small group of people to fight. He wasn't really a warrior though. He died soon after he arrived. But he had started a revolution. Cuba later became free because of his ideas.

Ruben Salazar

Ruben Salazar fought for Mexican Americans' **civil rights**. He was born in Mexico in 1928. Then he moved to Texas with his family when he was very little.

Salazar joined the army. Then he went to college for **journalism**. He started working for newspapers. He wrote a lot about Mexicans living near the border. This was news for most people. The people who read his stories had never realized before what Mexicans were going through.

Salazar earned some awards for his writing and his TV spots. He spoke out for Mexican rights. He especially didn't like how the police treated Mexican-Americans.

One day, Salazar was covering **protests.** People were protesting the Vietnam War. He and his crew went into a bar. The police surrounded the bar. They threw tear gas canisters in. No one really knows why. One of the canisters hit Salazar in the head and he died.

People remember Salazar for his brave journalism. He wasn't afraid to tell people the truth.

Ernesto "Che" Guevara

Che Guevara might be the most famous Latino ever. You might have seen pictures of his face on T-shirts. His face is also on posters. It's painted on city walls. Che is a legend with Latinos and non-Latinos alike.

Che was born in Argentina in 1928. He couldn't go to school because he had bad **asthma**. He had to learn at home. His mother taught him how to read and write. He was smart, and he learned a lot.

When Che was older, he went to college to study medicine. While he was in college, he traveled around Argentina on his motorcycle. He saw that a lot of people were poor. He wanted to help all those poor people.

After he graduated, he went to Guatemala. There was a revolution

Journalism *is writing news stories for magazines and newspapers.*

Protests *are when people speak out against the government.*

Asthma *is a disease that makes it hard for a person to breath because the tubes in their lungs get too narrow to let air in and out.*

there. People wanted change. He signed up as an army doctor. The side he was fighting for lost. Che fled to Mexico.

Then Che met Fidel Castro. Castro is the man who led the revolution in Cuba. Che liked Castro's ideas. The revolution wanted to make poor people's lives better. Che wanted to help him overthrow the government in Cuba, which was hurting people. He offered to be a doctor for Castro's army.

Guevara and the Cuban flag on buildings in Cuba

Che and Castro and a small group went to Cuba. They were attacked and they lost. They didn't give up. They hid. They convinced people to join them. Slowly, people joined their cause. And then, years later, they won. They overthrew the government that had been so cruel to people.

After Castro won and became Cuba's leader, he gave Che a good government job. But Guevara didn't like working in an office. He wanted to be out talking to people. He wanted to be fighting revolutions.

So he went to Bolivia. He helped Bolivians fight their own revolution. He lived in the jungle, fighting.

In 1967, Che Guevara was captured. By now, everyone knew who he was. He was a hero to some. Others didn't like him very much. The Bolivian army had him put to death.

Che Guevara is still very famous. Some people admire his commitment to the poor. He chose to live a poor life. He didn't become rich. He did his own work for himself. He went without food if he had to.

On the other hand, Che Guevara encouraged violence. He believed that violence was the only way to change things. Many Cuban Americans remember that he killed people after he and Castro won.

The Mirabal Sisters

Dominicans remember four sisters who helped stop a **dictator** in the Dominican Republic. They are Patria, Minerva, María Teresa, and Bélgica Mirabal.

The dictator Rafael Trujillo ruled the country. He kept people poor. He killed people.

The Mirabal sisters grew up in a rich family. They had a lot of powerful friends. They saw that Trujillo was bad for the country. The sisters agreed that he needed to leave.

They organized a secret group. They called it Las Mariposas (The Butterflies). The group fought Trujillo.

Trujillo found out. He arrested the sisters' husbands. They were put in jail. The sisters went to visit their husbands one day. Bélgica stayed behind to watch their children. The other three drove in a car. On the way, Trujillo's men stopped the car. They killed the three sisters.

Their death made people very angry. Dominicans started a revolution. Eventually, Trujillo was gone. The Mirabal sisters had inspired a lot of change, both with their lives and with their deaths. They were very brave.

Inspiration

All of these heroes **inspire** Latinos today. Latin America has had lots of troubles. But it has also had a lot of people who are willing to fight for what is right. These people give Latinos today hope. Their stories make modern Latinos stronger.

> A **dictator** is someone who has complete control over a country's government.
>
> To **inspire** means to give someone strength, excitement, and new ideas.

chapter 4
RELIGION

Religion is important to a lot of Latinos. Most are Christians. They read the Bible, go to church, and believe in God.

More than half of Latinos are Catholic. That's one kind of Christian. Many others are Pentecostal. That's another type of Christian.

There are also Latinos who aren't Christian at all. A few are Jewish or Muslim or Buddhist. Some practice Native religions.

Changes in Religion

Before Columbus and the Europeans came, the people who already lived in the Americas had their own religions. Their religions were different from European religions.

> To **convert** means to change the way someone thinks. It can mean to persuade someone to believe in a certain religion.

Right away, when the Europeans came, they tried to **convert** the Natives. They didn't understand the Native religions. They didn't want to understand them! The Europeans wanted the Natives to be Christians like they were. Not many Natives wanted to convert, though.

The Europeans did awful things to the Natives. Why would anyone want to follow their religion?

But most Latinos today are Christian. They eventually lost their Native religions. How did that happen?

Some people were forced to convert. Others decided they liked Christianity over time. Many of the Catholic priests and monks helped the Native people. The Virgin of Guadalupe is another reason. Her story convinced a lot of Latinos to become Catholic.

The Virgin of Guadalupe

One day, in 1531 in Mexico, a man named Juan Diego was out walking. Juan Diego was Christian, but he was also a Native from the group called the Aztecs. Suddenly, he saw the Virgin Mary. She was surrounded by light.

The Virgin Mary had dark skin. She looked Aztec. She told Juan that she was the mother of God. She said that everyone should believe in her. It didn't matter if they were Aztec or European. She wanted to help everyone.

Juan was amazed. He went and found a church leader called a bishop. The bishop didn't believe him. He told Juan he would need a sign in order to believe him.

The image of the Virgin of Guadalupe appears on billboards, storefronts, and restaurants.

Soon after, Juan saw the Virgin Mary again. She told him to take off his cape and fill it with flowers. He did that. Then he took the cape to the bishop. He shook the flowers out of the cape. A picture of the Virgin Mary was left behind on the cape.

Now the bishop was convinced. He built a church for Mary in Mexico City. It was called Guadalupe.

The Virgin of Guadalupe convinced many people in Latin America to become Catholic. Her message told them that Christianity wasn't just a white man's religion. It was for everyone. And Latinos now had their own special way to come to God, through the Virgin of Guadalupe.

Pentecostals

It used to be that almost all Latinos were Catholics. That was the only kind of Christian there was in Latin America.

Then some became Pentecostal. The first Pentecostal church was in Los Angeles, California, in 1906.

The Pentecostals believe in a personal connection with God. They encourage people to talk to God. They also "speak in tongues." That means they believe God helps them speak in other languages. It's a sign of their personal connection with God.

A street mural expresses the faith of Latino Pentecostals.

Religion Today

Almost half of all Catholics are Latinos. They're an important part of the Catholic Church.

Latinos bring their own flavor to their religion. Catholics have masses, where the Bible is read and the priest speaks. Masses are traditionally very serious. Latino masses are livelier. People play the guitar and clap their hands. It's more like a party.

All Catholics believe in the Virgin Mary, the mother of Jesus. Latinos especially love her. Her picture appears everywhere. She's on the walls of stores and homes. She is on shirts. On bumper stickers and flags. And on candles. Her image can be found on just about everything. She's always wearing a blue cape. She is smiling.

A Helping Hand

Latino churches think it's important to help other people. It doesn't matter what kind of church it is. Catholics and Pentecostals and others all work to help others in need.

Churches do a lot of things to make people's lives better. They help kids leave gangs. They help people find jobs. They set up kitchens to feed the hungry.

Statue of the Virgin Mary.

One church in Santa Ana, California, is a good example of this. First, church members set up a food warehouse. They got donations from grocery stores. The church fed hundreds of people every week. But so many more people were hungry.

The church set up something called the Kingdom Coalition. Sixty different churches belong. Together, they help many, many people. They give them food, education, and other things.

OTHER RELIGIONS

Not all Latinos are Christians. Almost a million Cubans, Puerto Ricans, and Dominicans practice *Santeria*. The Africans who used to be slaves brought this religion from the Yoruba tribe in Africa. Now some Latinos believe in it too.

Thousands of Latinos have also converted to Islam. Many people used to be Muslim in Spain. Then the Christian king and queen made them stop being Muslim. For some Latinos, Islam is a rediscovery of long-lost roots.

Traditional Native beliefs also appeal to many Latinos. Some very ancient practices are still followed by *curanderas*, or traditional healers.

CROSSING POINT
WELCOME
VISA
FREE TOURIST MAPS
BOUNDARY
OF THE
UNITED STATES
TREATY OF
RE-ESTABLISHED
BY TREATIES OF

chapter 5
IMMIGRATION

Thousands of people immigrate to the United States every year. Some do it legally. Some do it illegally.

Not everyone who wants to come to the United States can. The United States doesn't let just anyone live here. The government has rules about who can and who can't. All together, the rules are called "immigration policy." (A policy is a government's way of doing something.)

The rules are very complicated. They change all the time. There's a lot of fighting about immigration policy. One group wants the United States to welcome more people. Another group wants the United States to keep more people out. People argue about it. People on each side have their own reasons for thinking the way they do.

There are a lot of reasons for letting people into the United States. The world is all connected. It's hard to keep people in one country. They move around all the time. The United States also has a lot of money. It has a lot more money than most other countries. Some people think we should share it with whoever wants to come here. These people think that people are people, no matter where they come from, and that we should all share with each other. People in favor of allowing immigration also believe that immigrants are good for the country. They do important jobs that other Americans don't want to do. They buy goods and help businesses make money. They bring interesting art and music and ways of doing things to America.

But other people say that the United States already has all the people it needs. These people think that more people would be bad for America.

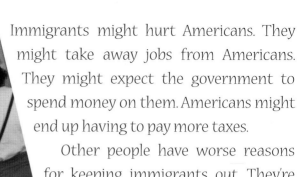

Immigrants might hurt Americans. They might take away jobs from Americans. They might expect the government to spend money on them. Americans might end up having to pay more taxes.

Other people have worse reasons for keeping immigrants out. They're afraid of people who are different from them. Immigrants often speak other languages. They belong to different cultures. They look different.

But **racism** is a bad reason for keeping people out of the United States!

The United States has created a system of controlling who is allowed to come to America and who isn't. People from other countries who come to the United States have to have a passport. They get their passport stamped when they go through the airport or cross a border in their cars. This way the U.S. government knows who is entering the country.

Immigrants don't just want to visit the United States, though. They want to live here. If you come to the United States for anything other than a vacation, you have to have something called a visa. You apply for a visa before you come to the United States. You have to prove you are who you say you are. A visa lets you into the United States.

Another document called a green card lets you stay in the United States. People with visas can apply for green cards if they want to live in the United States for a long time.

Some people want to become citizens. Then they can live permanently in the United States. Green cards and visas don't last forever. Citizenship does. Citizens have all the

> **Racism** *is the belief that people with one color of skin are better and smarter than people whose skin is a different color. Racism is wrong!*

rights that anyone else has in the United States. They can vote.

To become a citizen, you have to be able to speak English. You take a test to prove you know the language and that you know something about American history.

If you pass, you attend a swearing-in ceremony. Then you're a citizen!

Illegal Immigration

Getting to the United States legally can be hard. Visas and green cards are hard to get. But some people really want to come here. So they come illegally. They come without the U.S. government's permission.

People who immigrate illegally to the United States have to really want to come. They have to want to cross a desert and get past the immigration officials.

They don't bother to wait years and years for a green card. They need to come now. Maybe they need to make money for family back home. Or their families already live in the United States. Or they want to get away from a bad situation in their home country. Or they can't find work at home and they think they'll be able to in the United States.

Tijuana's slums crowd up against the U.S.-Mexican border.

There are probably about 11 million illegal immigrants in the United States. There could be as many as 20 million! A lot of them come from Latin America. And a lot of those come from Mexico.

Getting across the border is dangerous. Most Latino immigrants try to cross over the Mexican-United States border. Some of the border is walled off. There's barbed wire in other places. There are helicopters looking for illegal immigrants. There are border police.

A lot of the border isn't watched all the time. But those parts of the border are mostly desert. Illegal immigrants cross the desert to get to the United States.

Most immigrants hire a coyote. Coyotes are guides. They know the best way to get across the border. The catch is that you have to pay for a coyote. Each person has to pay at least a couple thousand dollars. That's a lot of money for most immigrants.

Then the coyote takes them across. The coyote might put the people all in a van and smuggle them over the border. That's dangerous because there isn't enough air in the vans. People have died doing that.

LATINOS TODAY

HOW TO BECOME A U.S. CITIZEN

To become a U.S. citizen, you have to live in the country for five years (three years to get a green card, then two more after that). You also have to meet the following qualifications:

• be at least eighteen years old

• never have committed a crime

• be able to prove you've lived for five years in the United States

• be able to speak English

• be able to pass a basic test of American government, history, and culture

Or the coyote might lead them by foot. A bunch of immigrants all walk together through the desert and across the border. It's hot. There isn't any water. They could get lost. People die that way too.

Even if everyone is safe, border crossers often get caught. Then they are sent back to their country. They don't get their money back from the coyote.

Some immigrants try again and again. It takes most people two or more tries to get across.

Even if immigrants get across, life isn't easy once they reach the United States. It's hard to get a good job when you're illegal. People aren't

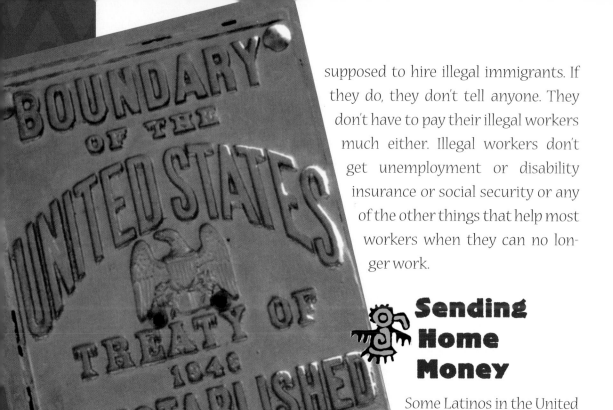

supposed to hire illegal immigrants. If they *do*, they don't tell anyone. They don't have to pay their illegal workers much either. Illegal workers don't get unemployment or disability insurance or social security or any of the other things that help most workers when they can no longer work.

Sending Home Money

Some Latinos in the United States still talk to their families in other countries. This is especially true for immigrants who came to the United States not too long ago.

One main reason that Latinos come to the United States is to make money for their families. They want to find jobs. Then they send the money they make to people back home.

Sometimes only one person in a family immigrates. He only wants to make money to send back. Then he'll go back to his family. Other people bring some family members with them but leave some behind.

Every month, people send money to their families. It could be just a few dollars. Or it could be $300 or more. That amount of money in the United States won't last long. But in Guatemala or Colombia, it's a lot of money.

People feel good when they can help their families. But sending their money home also means they have less to spend on themselves. If Latinos send too much back home, they don't have enough in the United States. They can't afford an apartment. Or enough food.

Eventually some people make enough money to bring their families here. Then they can start new lives together.

Money from relatives in the United States allows a family in Tijuana to install a system for running water.

chapter 6
SPANISH, ENGLISH, OR BOTH?

All those Latino immigrants are bringing something with them—Spanish. And they're still speaking it in the United States.

But not everyone likes that. Should Spanish speakers learn English? If so many Americans are Latino, should all Americans speak both English and Spanish? Should we even bother to teach English?

Which language would be better for Americans to use? Which language would help new immigrants more?

People get into arguments about these questions.

Spanish-Speakers

Spanish is the second-most common language in the United States. Probably about 40 million people speak it at home. Lots more can use it whenever they want.

But most of those people also know English. Most Latinos can speak English very well. Some are still learning. Older people are more likely not to know English. It's harder for older people to learn a new language.

Spanish is everywhere in the United States. Stores have Spanish names. Companies advertise in Spanish. Products have Spanish labels. Street signs are in Spanish.

In certain neighborhoods you can't even find much English. Lots of Latinos live there—and the businesses there have noticed! They want their customers to be able to understand what they're selling and feel welcome.

Bilingual Education

Cubans changed how schools were run in Florida. Lots of Cubans came to the state. They brought their children with them. The Cubans mostly spoke Spanish.

People welcomed Cubans. They wanted to help them. Florida set up a system of **bilingual** education. Half the school day was in English. The other half was in Spanish. That way, everyone could learn. And everyone learned a new language.

Other states copied Florida. Texas and other states started bilingual programs. They thought it was the best way to help Latino students.

Pretty soon the U.S. government stepped into the picture. It set aside money to pay for bilingual education all over the country.

> **Bilingual** *means that something or someone has two languages.*

Soon, the government said that schools *had* to have bilingual education. If there were a lot of students who didn't speak English, their schools had to have bilingual programs.

Not everyone liked that. Some teachers thought there were better ways of educating Spanish-speaking students. Bilingual education wasn't perfect. These teachers wanted non-English speaking kids to succeed. They didn't think bilingual programs were teaching students what they needed to know to do well in American life.

People did some studies. Sometimes bilingual schools worked. Sometimes they didn't.

Most Latinos like bilingual education. Their kids can learn English. But they can also hold on to Spanish.

Other ways of education can be more stressful. It's hard for a kid to only learn in English if she can't understand English. She won't learn very fast. She might even fail or drop out of school.

Some Latinos do like English-only schools. They think it's the only way that their kids will learn English, and learn it fast. With bilingual education, they might learn only enough English to get by. But they won't be **fluent**. So not even Latinos agree on this issue!

English Only

Some people in the United States want to protect English. They think that Spanish threatens America's special **identity**. They want everyone to speak English.

Thirty-one states have made English the **official** language. That doesn't mean that everyone has to speak English all the time. It does mean that everything the government does is in English.

The United States as a whole doesn't have an official language. Some people think that English should be America's official language.

In a few states, people have voted on making English the only language taught in schools. In California, kids can only get one year of bilingual education. Then they are taught in English.

Both

Then there are people who think that Americans should know more than one language. We should speak English. And another language. It might as well be Spanish.

People in other countries usually speak more than one language. In parts of Europe, for example, people speak two, three, or more languages. Let's say you live in Sweden. You know Swedish. You probably also learned English. And you know another language like French or Spanish or German.

Fluent *means that you can speak quickly and easily.*

Identity *is all the special things that make a person or a country what it is.*

Official *means that something has been approved by the government.*

ENGLISH, SPANISH . . . OR SPANGLISH?!

Spanish expressions are heard more and more in the English language of the United States. At the same time, English influences the language of Spanish-speaking Latinos. It is not uncommon for Latinos to slip "Spanglish" words into their talk. These are words that mix the two languages together. Some examples:

• *espelear*—to spell

• *lonche*—lunch

• *la marketa*—the market

• *¡Catchalo!*—Catch it!

A Cuban student demonstrates his national pride in this drawing.

Maybe you even know two other languages. All together, you speak three, four, or more languages.

The United States is unusual in that we only learn English. Sometimes we learn another language in high school. But we don't really speak it well.

This could be a good opportunity for us to learn two languages. Since so many people speak Spanish, why don't we all learn it? What do you think?

SPANISH, ENGLISH, OR BOTH?

chapter 7
BUSINESS

Goya Foods is an American success story. It started with a man named Prudencio Unanue. He moved from Spain to Puerto Rico in 1902. Then he moved to New York City.

Prudencio wanted to buy his favorite foods in New York. He couldn't find them. He also saw that the Puerto Rican population was growing. Maybe they missed their favorite foods too. So he decided to start his own business.

He called his business Goya Foods. He sold Latino foods to Puerto Rican grocery stores. Soon, the company had a whole warehouse.

In 1976, Prudencio's son Joseph took over. He decided to sell to other Latinos, not just Puerto Ricans. He sold more than 800 different things.

Goya Foods made millions of dollars each year. Joseph started selling things to non-Latinos too. Goya could be found in all the big supermarkets.

Prudencio's son Andy is in charge now. Goya Foods is the biggest Latino-owned company in the United States. Thousands of employees work for Goya around the world.

The Good News

Goya Foods is just one example of a successful Latino business. There are many, many more businesses owned by Latinos. More than two million Latino businesses are in the United States. There are more all the time.

Starting a business is a good job choice for lots of people. Some Latinos want to be their own bosses. They want to start a small business.

A Latino business could be anything. It could be a restaurant. It could be a construction company. It could be a computer company. It all depends on who is starting the business.

Of course, you need money to start a business. Some Latinos don't have enough. They work for a while and save up. Then they start a business.

Latinos can get some help to start a business. The government offers money for people to start businesses. Other organizations do too. They may loan money. They teach people how to start a business. They help business owners get customers. Sometimes it's Latinos who help other Latinos.

Banks are starting to see that Latino businesses are important. Some have set aside some money just for Latino businesses. These banks offer Latino businesses loans. They also offer business advice.

The "bodega" is the traditional door for immigrants into the American economy.

Latino businesses in New York City

Most Latino businesses are small. Most often, they are *bodegas* (small grocery stores). Restaurants, clothing stores, and repair shops are also common.

Latino businesses do well in part because there are so many Latino customers. Latinos want to buy things. All together, Latinos can spend billions of dollars.

> **Discrimination** *is when someone is treated unfairly because of the color of her skin, her religion, or something else about her that sets her apart.*

The Bad News

At the same time, not all the news is good. Many Latinos are poor. They don't make much money. They worry about feeding their families and paying rent. That means they don't have a lot of extra money to buy things.

Two things get in the way of Latinos getting better-paying jobs. One is bad education. Schools with lots of Latinos often aren't very good. They're run down. They have big classes. There isn't enough money to buy things like computers.

Many Latinos don't even make it to graduation. They drop out first. And very few go on to college.

The other problem is **discrimination**. Latinos apply for a lot of jobs. Sometimes they don't get them just because they're Latino. Or they don't get paid enough because they're Latino. That's illegal. But it still happens.

chapter 8
THE FUTURE

Everyone in the United States helps to make the country what it is. Immigrants from Britain and Germany helped to form the United States. So did West Africans, the French, and Native Americans. Immigrants from Ireland and Italy added their own influences. Then Eastern Asians, Indians, and others added theirs. And Latinos have had a big part in building America.

Every culture has something to add to American culture. All together, we make up one country. But we can all hang on to our individual identities too.

Latinos have a big influence on the United States. They're the fastest growing group in the country. All those Latino immigrants have brought their cultures with them. Because there are so many Latinos in the United States, the United States has changed.

But that's okay! Americans now eat Mexican-inspired food. They hear Spanish on the street. They enjoy Latino art. There's nothing wrong with change. America has been changing ever since it was born!

Strength

Latinos want to keep their cultures strong. They teach their children Spanish. They go to festivals that celebrate their cultures. They teach other people about their cultures. All those things help keep their identities alive.

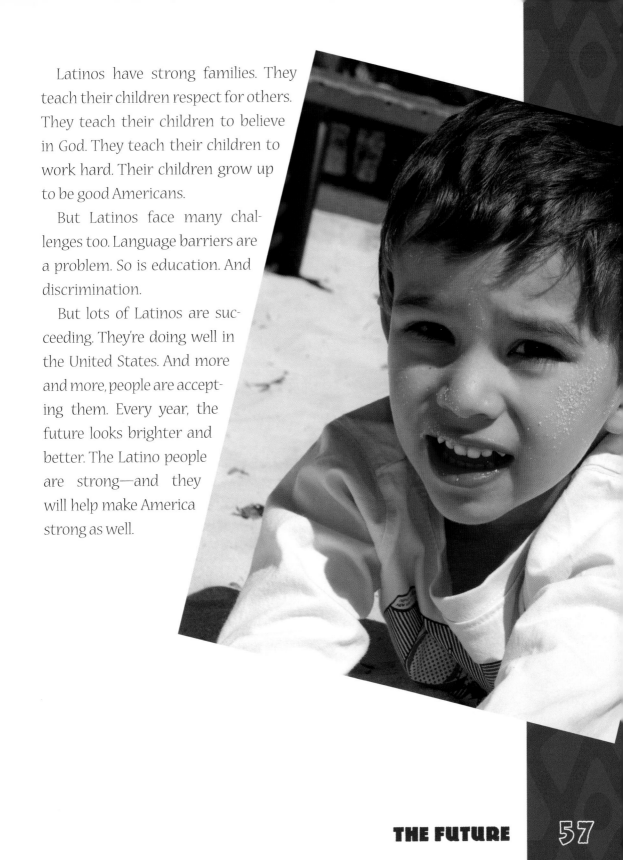

Latinos have strong families. They teach their children respect for others. They teach their children to believe in God. They teach their children to work hard. Their children grow up to be good Americans.

But Latinos face many challenges too. Language barriers are a problem. So is education. And discrimination.

But lots of Latinos are succeeding. They're doing well in the United States. And more and more, people are accepting them. Every year, the future looks brighter and better. The Latino people are strong—and they will help make America strong as well.

Time Line

1100 Mayan Civilization is at its strongest in Central America.

1325 Aztecs conquer Mexico.

1438 Inca rule begins in Peru.

1492 Christopher Columbus lands on the island of Hispaniola (Santo Domingo and Haiti).

1503 Hernan Cortes arrives in Hispaniola.

1521 Cortes defeats the Aztecs in Mexico.

1532 Francisco Pizarro conquers the Inca in Peru.

1610 Santa Fe, New Mexico, is built.

1690 First Spanish settlement in Texas is built.

1769 Franciscan missionary Junípero Serra builds the first mission in California. He will eventually build ten missions up and down California.

1817 Simón Bolívar begins his fight for independence from Spain in Colombia, Venezuela, and Ecuador.

1821 Mexico declares independence from Spain.

1845 Texas becomes part of the United States.

1846 Mexican-American War begins. New Mexico (which includes modern-day New Mexico, Arizona, southern Colorado, southern Utah, and southern Utah) becomes part of the United States.

1868 The Fourteenth Amendment to the U.S. Constitution says that all Hispanics born in the United States are U.S. citizens.

1898 Puerto Rico and Cuba become part of the United States.

1901 Cuba becomes an independent country.

1902 The Reclamation Act is passed, and takes away land from many Hispanic Americans.

1910 The beginning of the Mexican Revolution sends thousands of Mexicans north to settle in the American Southwest.

1943 U.S. government allows Mexican farmworkers to enter the United States.

1959 Fidel Castro takes over Cuba. Many Cubans immigrate to the United States.

1970s Violence in Central America spurs massive migration to the United States.

1990 President George Bush appoints the first woman and first Hispanic surgeon general of the United States: Antonia C. Novello.

2003 Hispanics are pronounced the nation's largest minority group surpassing African Americans—after new Census figures are released showing the U.S. Hispanic population at 37.1 million as of July 2001.

2006 According to the Census Bureau, the number of Hispanic-owned businesses grew three times faster than the national average for all U.S. businesses.

Find Out More

IN BOOKS

Laezman, Rick. *100 Hispanic-Americans Who Shaped American History*. San Mateo, Calif.: Bluewood Books, 2001.

Novas, Himilce. *Everything You Need to Know About Latino History*. New York: Plume, 2008.

Ochoa, George. *Amazing Hispanic American History: A Book of Answers for Kids.* New York: Wiley, 2008.

Petrillo, Valerie. *A Kid's Guide to Latino History*. Chicago: Chicago Review Press, 2009.

ON THE INTERNET

Celebrating Hispanic Heritage
www.timeforkids.com/news/celebrating-hispanic-heritage/13261

Hispanic Heritage Activities
www.nickjr.com/printables/all-shows/seasonal_hispanic-heritage/
all-ages/index.jhtml

Latino Children's Culture
www.unc.edu/world/latin_am_resources.shtml

Picture Credits

Benjamin Stewart: p. 10, 23, 32, 35, 38, 39, 42, 43, 51, 53, 55

Comstock: p. 47

Corbis: p. 13, 14

Cuban Art Space, Center for Cuban Studies: p. 49

Jeff Whyte | Dreamstime.com: p. 28

Juan Camilo Bernal | Dreamstime.com: p. 40

Library of Congress, Prints & Photographs Division: p. 24

Lyricmac: p. 25

MK Bassett-Harvey: p. 8, 12, 22, 30, 36, 44, 50, 54

Monkey Business Images | Dreamstime.com: p. 20, 57

Photos.com: p. 46

Robert Bayer | Dreamstime.com: p. 56

Stavros Damos | Dreamstime.com: p. 18

Stephen Finn | Dreamstime.com: p.17

The Records of the Offices of the Government of Puerto Rico in the U.S., Centro de Estudios Puertorriqueños, Hunter College, CUNY, Photographer unknown: p. 52

Zhanglianxun | Dreamstime.com: p. 34

Index

About the Author and the Consultant

Thomas Arkham has studied history for most of his life. He is an editor, author, and avid collector who lives in Upstate New York.

Dr. José E. Limón is professor of Mexican-American Studies at the University of Texas at Austin where he has taught for twenty-five years. He has authored over forty articles and three books on Latino cultural studies and history. He lectures widely to academic audiences, civic groups, and K–12 educators.